TEACHING TOWN
EARLY LEARNING ALL AROUND THE TOWN

Written and Compiled by Elizabeth McKinnon
Illustrated by Susan Dahlman

Warren Publishing House
Everett, Washington

We wish to thank the following teachers, childcare workers, and parents for contributing some of the activities in this book: Valerie Bielsker, Olathe, KS; Janice Bodenstedt, Jackson, MI; Jan Brummell, Lawrence, KS; Cindy Dingwall, Palatine, IL; Susan M. Paprocki, Northbrook, IL; Susan Peters, Upland, CA; Diane Thom, Maple Valley, WA.

Editorial Staff
Managing Editor: Kathleen Cubley
Contributing Editors: Gayle Bittinger, Kate Ffolliott, Susan Hodges, Jean Warren
Copy Editor: Mae Rhodes
Proofreader: Kris Fulsaas
Editorial Assistant: Kate Ffolliott

Design and Production Staff
Art Manager: Jill Lustig
Book Design: Lynne Faulk
Layout Production: Sarah Ness
Cover Design: Brenda Mann Harrison
Cover Illustration: Susan Dahlman
Production Manager: JoAnna Brock

ISBN 1-57029-068-7

Library of Congress Catalog Number 95-60511
Printed in the United States of America
Published by: Warren Publishing House
            P.O. Box 2250
            Everett, WA 98203

20 19 18 17 16 15 14 13 12 11 10 9 8 7 6 5 4 3 2 1

INTRODUCTION

Whether you are weighing vegetables at the grocery store or mailing packages at the post office, you can turn your town into a teaching town just by making use of ordinary items in ordinary places.

Every busy parent has experienced taking a child on errands only to have the child become bored and frustrated. Don't despair—relief is on the way! With *Teaching Town* as your resource, you will begin to view shopping and the running of other errands through your child's eyes.

Children see such trips as adventures. They enjoy exploring locations as much as seeing new things and people. The simple process of snacking at a restaurant or buying clothing at a department store can become fun for your child if you take the opportunity to slow down and really let him or her learn from the experience.

Trying one or two of the activities in this book when visiting different areas of your town can enrich routine errands for both you and your child.

Teaching Town is divided into ten chapters: Grocery Store, Post Office, Bank, Library, Hardware Store, Restaurant, Garden Store, Department Store, Doctor's Office, and Gas Station.

Each chapter contains fun, easy activities to do at the location, followed by related activities that you and your child can do when you return home. The activities are grouped into the areas of language, creativity, thinking skills, coordination, science, and self-awareness.

At first glance, these activities may seem to be "just play." However, as the introductory sentences to the activities explain, each activity uses a specific skill—one that forms part of a foundation necessary for higher learning.

For instance, participating in dramatic-play and oral-language activities prepares your child for communicating clearly with others. Art projects spark the imagination needed for effective reading, writing, and scientific speculation. Playing matching and sorting games develops an understanding of likes and differences, a skill used in nearly all learning areas, including math, science, reading, and writing.

Also, small-muscle coordination activities pave the way for learning how to use a pen or pencil; science activities promote thinking skills; and self-esteem activities lead to building self-confidence, so necessary for your child's success in all learning areas.

Since you are your child's first teacher, use the opportunity of daily outings to start teaching him or her basic skills and concepts. Just open to a page for one of the errands you plan to do today, skim through the easy step-by-step instructions, and begin!

A WORD ABOUT SAFETY

All the activities in *Teaching Town* are appropriate for the ages listed. However, keep in mind that when doing the activities, an adult should supervise to make sure that children do not put materials or objects into their mouth.

As for art materials, such as scissors, glue, or felt tip markers, use those that are specifically labeled as safe for children unless the materials are to be used only by an adult.

CONTENTS

GROCERY STORE 7

POST OFFICE 25

BANK 43

LIBRARY 57

HARDWARE STORE 73

RESTAURANT 87

GARDEN STORE 101

DEPARTMENT STORE 117

DOCTOR'S OFFICE 133

GAS STATION 147

INDEX 158

GROCERY PICTURE LIST

*Your child will **enjoy helping you shop** with **this prereading activity**.*

GROCERY STORE

AGES
3 to 5

YOU WILL TEACH
Language

YOU WILL NEED
paper
pen
grocery items

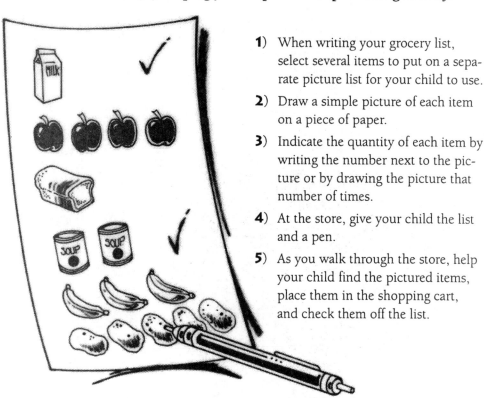

1) When writing your grocery list, select several items to put on a separate picture list for your child to use.

2) Draw a simple picture of each item on a piece of paper.

3) Indicate the quantity of each item by writing the number next to the picture or by drawing the picture that number of times.

4) At the store, give your child the list and a pen.

5) As you walk through the store, help your child find the pictured items, place them in the shopping cart, and check them off the list.

LETTERS EVERYWHERE

The grocery store is a great place to try this letter-recognition activity.

1) With your child, find a food package with the first letter of his or her name on it.

2) As you walk up and down the aisles, have your child look for other food packages that contain that letter.

3) Help your child find the letter on shelves, sale signs, or large signs overhead.

4) Follow the same procedure to look for other familiar letters.

COUPON MATCH

Let your child help you grocery shop with this matching activity.

GROCERY STORE

AGES
3 to 5

YOU WILL TEACH
Thinking Skills

YOU WILL NEED
grocery coupons
envelope
grocery products

1) Before going to the store, select several grocery coupons for products you want to buy.

2) Place the coupons in an envelope and give them to your child to carry.

3) When you get to the store, help your child look for the products that match the pictures on the coupons and place those items in the shopping cart.

4) Let your child give the coupons to the clerk when you reach the checkout stand.

ANOTHER IDEA: *Let your child use crayons or felt tip markers to decorate the envelope for carrying coupons. Save the envelope to use on future trips to the store.*

WHERE WOULD IT BE?

This classification activity demonstrates how grouping similar items together makes shopping easier.

1) When you are at the store, tell your child that you need a certain item, such as hot dog buns.

2) Ask your child if he or she thinks you should look for the buns in the meat section or the bread section.

3) After your child names a section, go there to let your child check his or her response.

4) Ask similar questions such as: "Should we look for yogurt in the cereal section or the milk section? Should we look for potatoes in the vegetable section or the juice section?"

5) Talk with your child about what would happen if all the products in a grocery store were mixed up together on the shelves. Would it be easier or harder to shop?

LARGE AND SMALL

Recognizing large and small sizes is part of this matching activity.

AGES
2 to 5

YOU WILL TEACH
Thinking Skills

YOU WILL NEED
canned fruits or vegetables

1) Take your child to the canned fruits or vegetables section.

2) From the shelf, take a large can and a small can of two different products, such as peaches and pineapple or beans and corn. (Make sure that each large and small can are from the same company and have matching labels.)

3) Mix up the cans and show them to your child.

4) Ask your child to find the large and small size of each canned product.

5) Replace the cans on the shelf and choose other sets of large and small cans, if you wish.

LET'S WEIGH THEM

This math activity involves using comparison skills.

1) Go with your child to the produce section.

2) Give your child a potato to hold in each hand.

3) Ask your child to tell you which potato feels heavier and which feels lighter.

4) Let your child help weigh each potato in the produce scale to check his or her responses.

5) Follow the same procedure using other vegetables or fruits, such as cucumbers, oranges, or apples.

GROCERY STORE

—

AGES
3 to 5

—

YOU WILL TEACH
Thinking Skills

—

YOU WILL NEED
potatoes
produce scale
other vegetables or fruits

13

COLORFUL SHOPPING

Grocery items provide many opportunities for color-recognition activities like this one.

GROCERY STORE

AGES
3 to 5

YOU WILL TEACH
Thinking Skills

YOU WILL NEED
various grocery items

14

1) As you walk through the store, ask your child to look for various colors.

2) Point out different colors of the same item, such as red and green grapes, green and yellow beans, and brown and white eggs.

3) Encourage your child to find other items that come in more than one color. What about juice? Cookies? Cheese?

HOW MANY INSIDE?

Your child will become more aware of the number of items in a package with this math activity.

1) Take your child to the egg section.

2) Open an egg carton and count the number of eggs inside, or count as you and your child fill a carton with eggs to purchase later.

3) Point to another carton and ask your child to guess how many eggs will be inside.

4) Open the carton and have your child help count the eggs to check his or her response.

5) Follow the same procedure with other packaged items, such as hot dogs, canned or bottled colas, or boxed juices. (Be sure to choose only those items that can be counted without destroying the packaging.)

GROCERY STORE

—

AGES
3 to 5

—

YOU WILL TEACH
Thinking Skills

—

YOU WILL NEED
*eggs in cartons
other packaged food items*

15

BAKERY FUN

This learning activity develops math skills as well as color- and shape-recognition skills.

GROCERY STORE

AGES
3 to 5

YOU WILL TEACH
Thinking Skills

YOU WILL NEED
fresh bakery goods

1) Take your child to the bakery display case.

2) Encourage your child to name the kinds of items in the case, such as cookies, doughnuts, and cakes.

3) Ask your child to do such things as the following.

- Count the number of bear cookies, jelly doughnuts, clown cupcakes, and so forth.

- Name the shapes of different cookies.

- Point to the yellow cakes, the green cookies, the doughnuts with red sprinkles, and so on.

ANOTHER IDEA: *Let your child choose one bakery item and order it from the salesclerk to buy and take home.*

IN-CART WAITING GAMES

Games like these use language skills, math skills, color-recognition skills, and shape-recognition skills.

1) When you are waiting in line at the checkout stand, let your child sit in the shopping cart and do activities like those that follow.

- Ask your child to point to and name each of the items in your cart.

- With your child, count the number of items in the cart.

- Have your child name a color that he or she is wearing. Ask him or her to point to items in the cart that are the same color.

- Ask your child to find an item that is round, square, or rectangular.

GROCERY STORE

AGES
2 to 5

YOU WILL TEACH
Thinking Skills

YOU WILL NEED
*shopping cart
grocery items*

I SEE SOMETHING

Try playing this problem-solving game while you are waiting in line with your child.

1) Select an item that you and your child can see.

2) Start describing the item to your child. For instance, if the item is a helium-filled birthday balloon, you might say, "I see something that floats in the air, is shiny, and has words on it."

3) Keep giving clues until your child guesses what the item is.

4) Let your child describe an item and have you guess what it is.

APPLE PRODUCTS

This science activity uses classification and comparison skills.

1) Take your child to the produce section and let him or her pick out an apple to buy and take home.

2) Talk about other foods that are made from apples.

3) Ask your child to tell you where you might find dried apples, applesauce, apple juice, and apple muffins.

4) Find the sections where these products are located and choose several of them to purchase.

5) At home, let your child sample the different apple products, encouraging him or her to tell you how the tastes compare.

ANOTHER IDEA: *Try this activity using another product such as corn.*

GROCERY STORE

AGES
3 to 5

YOU WILL TEACH
Science

YOU WILL NEED
apple products

LET'S PLAY GROCERY STORE

Your child will enjoy being a grocer with this dramatic-play activity.

1) Give your child a few sturdy fruits and vegetables, such as oranges or potatoes, to display on a low table.

2) To add to the display, give your child clean, empty food containers, such as cereal boxes, milk cartons, food cans, and frozen dinner boxes.

3) Provide several brown paper grocery bags, along with a shoebox for a cash register.

4) Let your child be the grocer while you take the role of customer, using store coupons or play money to "buy" different items.

5) Trade places and let your child be the customer.

PLAYDOUGH BAKERY

This art activity is always popular with young children.

1) Set out playdough along with a rolling pin, cookie cutters, small pans, a muffin tin, and a baking sheet.

2) Have your child roll out some of the playdough, cut out cookie shapes, and place them on the baking sheet.

3) Let your child use the rest of the playdough to make such things as muffins or cakes to "bake" in a pretend oven.

4) When the baked goods are "done," let your child place them in bakery boxes, if you wish.

ANOTHER IDEA: *Give your child such items as cookie sprinkles and birthday candles to use for decorating his or her baked goods.*

GROCERY STORE AT-HOME FUN

—

AGES
2 to 5

—

YOU WILL TEACH
Creativity

—

YOU WILL NEED
*playdough
rolling pin
cookie cutters
pans
bakery boxes (optional)*

21

BUYING AND SELLING

This simple activity helps develop math skills.

GROCERY STORE AT-HOME FUN

AGES
3 to 5

YOU WILL TEACH
Thinking Skills

YOU WILL NEED
empty food containers
pen
plain stickers
or masking tape
scissors
green paper

1) Select five empty food containers.

2) Using a pen, make five "price stickers" by writing the numbers 1 to 5 on plain stickers or pieces of masking tape.

3) Attach one price sticker to each food container.

4) Set out the containers and give your child 15 "dollar bills" cut from green paper.

5) Have your child identify the number on each container and give you that number of dollars to "buy" it.

6) When your child has purchased all the items, trade places and let your child be the seller.

AGE VARIATION: *For younger children, attach one to five stickers to the food containers. Have the children count the stickers on a container and hand you that many dollars to buy it.*

BAGGING GROCERIES

This activity helps develop eye-hand coordination while calling for the use of comparison skills.

1) Set out a variety of grocery items, such as a melon, a plastic bottle of juice, several cans of food, a box of dry cereal, a package of cookies, and a bag of chips.

2) Give your child a large brown paper grocery bag.

3) Let your child pack the grocery items in the paper bag, one at a time.

4) Encourage your child to think about which items are heavier and which are lighter. Which items should go in the bag last so that they do not get squashed or broken?

5) When the bag has been packed, let your child unpack it and help you put the items away.

GROCERY STORE AT-HOME FUN

—

AGES
2 to 5

—

YOU WILL TEACH
Coordination

—

YOU WILL NEED
grocery items
large grocery bag

POST OFFICE

POSTCARDS TO MAIL

This prereading-prewriting activity will encourage your child to keep an eye out for your mail carrier.

1) Before going to the post office, select a postcard to send to your child.

2) Let your child observe as you write a message, address the card, and stamp it.

3) Together, mail the postcard at the post office.

4) At home, watch with your child for the mail carrier to deliver the special mail.

5) Help your child "write" a postcard to mail to you.

6) Show your child the card when the mail carrier delivers it.

POSTCARD STORIES

Try this oral-language activity while you are waiting in line at the post office.

1) Have ready to mail several picture postcards that show familiar landmarks or other interesting scenes.

2) Give your child one of the postcards and ask him or her to describe the picture.

3) Give your child another postcard. Is the picture different from the one on the first postcard? In what ways?

4) Ask your child to pretend that he or she is in one of the postcard pictures. What things would he or she like to do there?

ANOTHER IDEA: *For a prewriting activity, help your child add his or her name to the postcards you are mailing.*

POST OFFICE

—

AGES
2 to 5

—

YOU WILL TEACH
Language

—

YOU WILL NEED
picture postcards

27

STAMP DESCRIPTIONS

For this listening game, use stamps on display at the post office.

POST OFFICE

⎯

AGES
3 to 5

⎯

YOU WILL TEACH
Language

⎯

YOU WILL NEED
postage stamps

1) Show your child several different postage stamps.

2) Ask your child to listen carefully while you begin to describe one of the stamps.

3) When your child recognizes which stamp you are describing, have him or her point to that stamp.

4) Let your child describe one of the stamps for you to identify.

WHICH IS HEAVIER?

Try this math game at the post office when you have packages to mail.

1) Prepare two packages for the mail.

2) At the post office, let your child hold first one package, then the other.

3) Ask your child to tell you which package is heavier and which is lighter.

4) Have your child check his or her responses by watching the postal clerk weigh the packages.

ANOTHER IDEA: *Ask your child which is heavier, a stamp or an apple? A shoe or a postcard? An envelope or a car?*

FUN IN LINE

This math game provides an enjoyable way to pass the time while waiting in line at the post office.

1) Call attention to people in line at the post office.

2) Ask your child to point out who is first in line and who is last.

3) Have your child count the people in line in ways such as those below.
   - people with packages
   - people with letters
   - people with packages and letters

ARRANGING LETTERS

Do this ordering activity at the post office when you have a number of letters to mail.

1) Give your child several letters of different sizes.

2) Ask your child to place the largest letter on your outstretched hands or a flat surface.

3) One at a time, have your child place the remaining letters on top of the first one, arranging them from largest to smallest.

POST OFFICE

AGES
2 to 5

YOU WILL TEACH
Thinking Skills

YOU WILL NEED
various sizes of letters

READY TO MAIL

This mailing activity helps develop eye-hand coordination.

POST OFFICE

AGES
3 to 5

YOU WILL TEACH
Coordination

YOU WILL NEED
addressed letters
postage stamps
mail slot

1) At the post office, give your child several letters addressed for mailing and a matching number of postage stamps.

2) Show your child where the stamps belong on the envelopes.

3) Let your child lick the stamps and stick them on the letters.

4) Help your child mail the letters, one at a time, in the mail slot or a mailbox.

LETTER BALANCE

Try this activity, which promotes small-muscle development, when you are waiting in line at the post office.

1) Ask your child to hold out his or her hand, palm down.

2) Place a letter on the back of your child's hand.

3) Have your child see how long he or she can balance the letter without letting it fall.

4) Let your child try balancing the letter on the opposite hand.

5) Have your child place the letter on your hand for you to balance.

POST OFFICE

—

AGES
3 to 5

—

YOU WILL TEACH
Coordination

—

YOU WILL NEED
letter

LET'S PLAY POST OFFICE

Your child is sure to enjoy this dramatic-play activity.

1) Make a pretend post office by first cutting a slit in a cardboard carton for a mailbox.

2) Using a low table for a counter, set out such items as stamplike stickers for stamps, junk mail, and several shoeboxes.

3) Using a felt tip marker, label the shoeboxes with different alphabet letters for sorting mail. Print matching letters on the junk mail envelopes.

4) With your child, do such activities as using play money to buy and sell the stamps, sorting the junk mail envelopes into the matching labeled boxes, and "writing" letters to stamp and mail in your pretend mailbox.

MAIL BAG

Your child takes the role of mail carrier in this dramatic-play activity.

1) Find a large manila envelope to use as a mail bag.

2) Use sharp scissors to poke a hole through each top corner of the envelope, just under the fold of the open flap.

3) Through the holes, tie the ends of a piece of yarn that has been cut to make a shoulder strap. Reinforce the holes with tape, if you wish.

4) Let your child decorate the bag with crayons or felt tip markers. Print "U.S. Post Office" on both sides.

5) Show your child how to put the bag over his or her shoulder.

6) Give your child pieces of junk mail to place in the bag and "deliver" to pretend addresses.

POST OFFICE AT-HOME FUN

AGES
3 to 5

YOU WILL TEACH
Language

YOU WILL NEED
large manila envelope
sharp scissors
yarn
tape (optional)
crayons or felt tip markers
junk mail

MAILBOX FUN

Listening to and following directions is the focus of this activity.

1) Give your child an assortment of envelopes and small index cards.

2) Let your child decorate the cards with felt tip markers and place the cards in the envelopes.

3) "Address" the envelopes by using felt tip markers to draw a simple picture, such as a banana, a square, or a flower, on the front of each one.

4) Use a knife to cut a slit in the lid of a shoebox to make a mailbox.

5) Give your child directions such as: "Mail the letter with a banana on it. Mail the letter with a square on it. Mail the letter with a red and blue flower on it."

6) When all the letters have been "mailed," empty the box and let your child give you directions for mailing.

STAMP PICTURES

This art activity provides a creative way to reuse colorful postage stamps.

1) Cut different kinds of canceled stamps from their envelopes.

2) Give your child the stamps, along with a piece of plain paper, glue, and felt tip markers.

3) Have your child glue the stamps on the paper any way he or she wishes.

4) Let your child use the markers to create a design on the paper that incorporates the stamps.

ANOTHER IDEA: *If you have a large number of stamps, let your child glue them all over a piece of paper to make a collage.*

AGES
3 to 5

YOU WILL TEACH
Creativity

YOU WILL NEED
*scissors
canceled postage stamps
paper
glue
felt tip markers*

MAIL MATCHUPS

This matching activity uses eye-hand coordination skills.

**POST OFFICE
AT-HOME FUN**

AGES
3 to 5

YOU WILL TEACH
Thinking Skills

YOU WILL NEED
*various envelopes
scissors
index cards or heavy paper*

1) Select four or five envelopes of different sizes.

2) For each envelope, cut an index card or a piece of heavy paper to fit exactly inside.

3) Set out the envelopes and cards.

4) Let your child try to fit the cards into the envelopes to find the matchups.

5) Keep the cards and envelopes in a large mailing envelope for your child to play with again another time.

MAILBOX SORTING GAME

This sorting activity can also be done with colors, numbers, or alphabet letters.

1) Make mailboxes by cutting a slit in the lids of two shoeboxes.

2) Using a felt tip marker, label each mailbox with a different shape, such as a square or a heart.

3) Make pieces of mail for each box by drawing a matching shape on the front of several sealed small envelopes.

4) Mix up the envelopes and let your child mail them in the appropriate mailboxes.

AGE VARIATION: *For older children, make the game more challenging by including three to five mailboxes.*

POST OFFICE AT-HOME FUN

AGES
2 to 5

YOU WILL TEACH
Thinking Skills

YOU WILL NEED
knife
shoeboxes
felt tip markers
small envelopes

STAMP LOTTO

Your child will enjoy playing this matching game.

**POST OFFICE
AT-HOME FUN**

—

AGES
2 to 5

—

YOU WILL TEACH
Thinking Skills

—

YOU WILL NEED
*canceled postage stamps
pen
index cards
glue*

1) Collect four different pairs of canceled postage stamps.

2) With a pen, divide two index cards into four sections each.

3) Glue one set of four postage stamps on one index card and the matching set of four stamps on the second card.

4) Cut one of the cards into four sections to make game pieces. Use the other card as a gameboard.

5) Mix up the game pieces and let your child place them on the matching sections of the gameboard.

AGE VARIATION: *For older children, include six to eight sections on the gameboard and make six to eight matching game pieces.*

MY OWN MAILBOX

This activity helps develop self-esteem by making your child feel special.

1) Select a half-gallon milk carton to use for making a mailbox for your child's room.

2) Wash and dry the milk carton and cut off the top.

3) Cover the outside of the carton by taping or gluing on construction paper.

4) Print your address on one side of the carton.

5) Use a brass paper fastener to attach a small flag shape cut from stiff red paper to the other side of the carton.

6) Let your child add decorations as he or she wishes.

7) Periodically, slip greeting cards, notes, and other "mail" into the mailbox for your child to discover.

POST OFFICE AT-HOME FUN

—

AGES
3 to 5

—

YOU WILL TEACH
Self-Awareness

—

YOU WILL NEED
half-gallon milk carton
scissors
construction paper
tape or glue
brass paper fastener
red paper flag shape
greeting cards or notes

DEPOSIT AND WITHDRAW

This vocabulary-building game is fun to play at the bank while you are waiting in line.

BANK

—

AGES
3 to 5

—

YOU WILL TEACH
Language

—

YOU WILL NEED
penny

1) Explain to your child that *deposit* means to put in and *withdraw* means to take out.

2) Give your child a penny.

3) Ask your child to deposit the penny in your hand and then withdraw it.

4) Continue by asking your child to deposit the penny in your other hand, your pocket, or your wallet and then withdraw it.

5) Let your child give you directions for depositing and withdrawing the penny.

BANK SLIPS

Your child will enjoy imitating you with this prereading-prewriting activity.

1) At the bank, let your child observe as you fill out a deposit slip. Explain what you are doing and why.

2) Give your child a blank deposit slip.

3) Let your child use a pen to "fill out" the deposit slip. (To make writing easier, you may wish to attach the slip to a small clipboard.)

4) When your child has finished, ask him or her to "read" the slip to you.

ANOTHER IDEA: *Follow the same procedure using withdrawal slips.*

BANK

—

AGES
3 to 5

—

YOU WILL TEACH
Language

—

YOU WILL NEED
deposit slips
pen
small clipboard (optional)

DOLLAR BILL FUN

This oral-language activity involves listening to and following directions.

BANK

AGES
3 to 5

YOU WILL TEACH
Language

YOU WILL NEED
dollar bill

1) When you are at the bank, show your child a dollar bill.

2) Ask your child to describe what he or she sees on the front of the bill.

3) Have your child point to such things as the picture of George Washington, a green letter or number, or the four number 1s.

4) Turn the bill over and ask your child to name the color on the back. Can he or she find a triangle or bird in the pictures? How many number 1s are on the back of the dollar bill?

NAMING COINS

Introduce your child to the names of coins with this vocabulary-building activity.

1) After asking a bank teller for some change, show your child a penny, a nickel, and a dime.

2) Encourage your child to touch and examine each coin as you name it.

3) Talk about the sizes and colors of the coins and point out the picture on each one.

4) Hand the coins to your child. Ask him or her to give you back the nickel, the penny, the dime.

5) Let your child ask you to hand over the coins as he or she names them.

AGE VARIATION: *For younger children, start with just two coins, such as a penny and a nickel, and gradually add other coins. For older children, start the game with a quarter added to the three coins.*

BANK
—
AGES
3 to 5
—
YOU WILL TEACH
Language
—
YOU WILL NEED
various coins

NUMBER SEARCH

Try this number-recognition activity while you are waiting in line at the bank.

BANK

—

AGES
3 to 5

—

YOU WILL TEACH
Thinking Skills

—

YOU WILL NEED
bank brochure
pen

48

1) Find a bank brochure that has numbers in it.

2) At the top of a page, write a number such as 2.

3) Show your child the number and together look for other 2s on the page.

4) Continue with other numbers from 1 to 5 that your child is familiar with, or let your child choose a number to search for on a page.

COUNTING IN LINE

This math activity helps pass the time while you are waiting in a long line.

1) With your child, count the number of people in line ahead of you.

2) Count how many leave the front of the line to go to teller windows.

3) Count the number of people who are left in line ahead of you now.

4) Have your child turn around and count the number of people who are waiting in line behind you.

ANOTHER IDEA: *Count the number of teller windows. How many are open? How many are closed?*

BANK

—

AGES
3 to 5

—

YOU WILL TEACH
Thinking Skills

—

YOU WILL NEED
line at a bank

WHAT DOESN'T BELONG?

Your child will enjoy playing this problem-solving game.

BANK

AGES
4 to 5

YOU WILL TEACH
Thinking Skills

YOU WILL NEED
bank interior

1) Have your child look around the bank while you talk about things you can see.

2) Also show your child money, checks, and deposit slips you use in bank transactions.

3) Say, "What does not belong in a bank—a penny, a desk, or an elephant?"

4) After your child responds, continue with similar examples such as: "A teller, a bus, or a deposit slip? A swing, a quarter, or a chair? A check, a dime, or a refrigerator?"

MY OWN ACCOUNT

Increase your child's self-esteem with this "grown-up" activity.

1) Ask at your bank about starting an account for your child (most banks will do this, requiring only a small initial deposit).

2) Start the account and show your child the passbook or other papers you receive.

3) Let your child make a small deposit in the account each time you do business at the bank.

4) When your child's account reaches an agreed upon amount, let him or her make a small withdrawal.

5) Keep the account active as long as you wish.

BANK

AGES
4 to 5

YOU WILL TEACH
Self-Awareness

YOU WILL NEED
money for deposit

LET'S PLAY BANK

You and your child will enjoy this dramatic-play activity.

BANK AT-HOME FUN

AGES
3 to 5

YOU WILL TEACH
Language

YOU WILL NEED
table
play money
muffin tin
pens
bank slips
old checks

1) Set out a table to use as a teller window.

2) On the table, let your child help arrange bank items, such as play money sorted into a muffin tin, pens, deposit and withdrawal slips, and old, blank checks.

3) Take turns with your child being the bank teller and the customer, doing tasks such as counting coins and bills, "filling out" bank slips for depositing and withdrawing money, and "writing" checks.

ANOTHER IDEA: *Use real coins to do activities that involve making change.*

COIN PURSE GAME

This sorting game involves following directions as well as using math skills.

1) In a coin purse, place several pennies, nickels, dimes, and quarters.

2) Give the coin purse to your child.

3) Let your child remove the coins from the purse one at a time, name them, and place them in four separate piles.

4) When all the coins are in piles, give your child directions such as: "Put three pennies into the purse. Put one quarter into the purse. Put two dimes into the purse."

5) Let your child give you directions for taking coins out of the purse and putting them back in.

BANK AT-HOME FUN

—

AGES
3 to 5

—

YOU WILL TEACH
Thinking Skills

—

YOU WILL NEED
coin purse
coins

SHINING PENNIES

This science activity makes pennies sparkle.

**BANK
AT-HOME FUN**

AGES
3 to 5

YOU WILL TEACH
Science

YOU WILL NEED
*tarnished pennies
small glass bowl
vinegar
salt
paper towel*

1) Show your child several tarnished copper pennies.

2) Set out a small glass bowl containing a mixture of ½ cup vinegar and 1 teaspoon salt.

3) Let your child drop the pennies into the mixture and watch as the tarnish disappears.

4) Remove the pennies from the bowl and let your child polish them with a paper towel.

5) Let your child save the shiny pennies or use them for playing bank games.

MY OWN BANK

Use this self-esteem activity to help your child begin to learn about saving money.

1) Find a can with a plastic lid to use for making a bank.

2) Cut a piece of construction paper to fit around the can.

3) Let your child use crayons or felt tip markers to decorate the paper.

4) Attach the paper to the outside of the can with tape or glue.

5) Use a sharp knife to cut a slit (large enough for coins to pass through) in the plastic lid of the can.

6) Place the lid on the can and give your child several coins to deposit in his or her bank.

7) Encourage your child to use the bank for saving money on a regular basis.

**BANK
AT-HOME FUN**

AGES
3 to 5

YOU WILL TEACH
Self-Awareness

YOU WILL NEED
*can with plastic lid
scissors
construction paper
crayons or felt tip markers
tape or glue
sharp knife
coins*

LOUD AND SOFT

Encourage appropriate library behavior with this vocabulary-building activity.

1) Before going to the library, talk with your child about *loud* and *soft*.

2) Find a music station on the radio. Turn the volume up and down, each time asking your child to tell you if the sound is loud or soft.

3) With your child, recite a nursery rhyme, such as "Mary Had a Little Lamb," first in a loud voice, then in a soft one.

4) Talk with your child about how soft voices are used at the library.

5) At the library, whenever necessary, use an agreed upon hand signal to remind each other to speak softly.

BOOK STORIES

Your child is sure to enjoy this prereading activity.

1) At the library, select a storybook that is unfamiliar to you and your child.

2) Together, "read" the book by looking at the illustrations and making up a story about what is in them.

3) Encourage your child to name the characters and describe what is happening in the illustrations.

4) After enjoying your own story, read the author's story with your child.

5) Ask your child to tell you which story he or she liked best.

LIBRARY

AGES
2 to 5

YOU WILL TEACH
Language

YOU WILL NEED
storybook

BOOK QUESTIONS

This prereading activity helps make books come alive for your child.

LIBRARY

AGES
2 to 5

YOU WILL TEACH
Language

YOU WILL NEED
storybook

1) Choose a storybook at the library.

2) As you read the book to your child, stop frequently to ask questions such as the following.

   • "What would you do if you were the story character?"

   • "Why do you think he or she is sad?"

   • "What made him or her do that?"

   • "What do you think will happen next?"

3) Ask similar questions whenever you read storybooks to your child.

COLOR SEARCH

This color-recognition activity encourages your child to become more aware of book illustrations.

1) Choose a color such as red.

2) With your child, look through a library picture book you have selected together.

3) Ask your child to point to and name red things in each illustration.

4) Follow the same procedure with a different color.

LIBRARY

AGES
2 to 5

YOU WILL TEACH
Thinking Skills

YOU WILL NEED
picture book

PAGE COUNT

This math activity uses comparison skills.

LIBRARY

—

AGES
3 to 5

—

YOU WILL TEACH
Thinking Skills

—

YOU WILL NEED
picture books

1) Find two short picture books of different lengths.

2) With your child, count the pages first in one book, then in the other.

3) Ask your child to tell you which book has the most pages and which has the fewest.

ANOTHER IDEA: *For a predicting activity, ask your child to guess which book will have the most pages before you count them.*

BOOK PILE

Encourage your child to help organize books on a library table with this ordering activity.

1) On a low library table, gather together four to six storybooks.

2) Ask your child to find the largest book and place it in front of you.

3) Have your child stack the remaining books on top of the first one from largest to smallest.

LIBRARY

—

AGES
2 to 5

YOU WILL TEACH
Thinking Skills

—

YOU WILL NEED
storybooks

BOOK BINGO

This classification activity uses prereading skills.

LIBRARY

—

AGES
3 to 5

—

YOU WILL TEACH
Thinking Skills

—

YOU WILL NEED
index card or heavy paper
pen
stickers
envelope

1) Divide a large index card or piece of heavy paper into nine sections.

2) In each section, print a topic, such as one of the following: "Family, Cars, Snow, Bugs, Moon, Alphabet, Trains, Nursery Rhymes, Baby Animals."

3) Place the card, along with nine stickers, in a large envelope and take it with you when you go to the library.

4) Help your child find a book that relates to one of the topics listed on the card and read the book together.

5) When you have finished the book, let your child attach a sticker to the appropriate section on the card.

6) Continue the activity on other days until all the sections have stickers.

Family	Moon	Bugs
Snow	Nursery Rhymes	Cars
Baby Animals	Trains	Alphabet

ABOUT ME

Use this self-esteem activity to help make the library experience a personal one for your child.

1) On each library visit, try one or more of the following ideas.

   • Have your child look through books to find a picture of a child who looks like him- or herself.

   • Ask your child to name one or two favorite books. Look for them together and check them out.

   • Talk about subjects that interest your child. Have him or her ask the librarian to help find a book about one of the topics.

2) When your child is old enough, let him or her talk to the librarian about getting a library card.

CHECK-OUT

LIBRARY

AGES
3 to 5

YOU WILL TEACH
Self-Awareness

YOU WILL NEED
library books
librarian

LET'S PLAY LIBRARY

In this dramatic-play activity, your child acts out the role of librarian.

1) Set out a low table for a library counter and a small bookcase with some of your child's storybooks arranged on the shelves.

2) Provide pretend library cards cut from posterboard and a dry rubber stamp.

3) With your child, take turns being the librarian, doing such tasks as helping to find books on the bookshelves, giving out library cards, pretending to stamp books (or run them through the computer), and putting "returned" books back onto the shelves.

READING CORNER

Help instill a love of books with this prereading activity.

1) Choose a corner of a room to be your child's special reading area.

2) Set out a small bookcase and fill it with storybooks.

3) Include a few floor pillows for your child to sit or lie on.

4) Keep the bookcase well stocked with new books and old favorites, and encourage your child to "read" one or more of them each day.

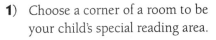

LIBRARY AT-HOME FUN

AGES
3 to 5

YOU WILL TEACH
Language

YOU WILL NEED
*small bookcase
storybooks
pillows*

READ ME A STORY

This prereading activity will encourage your child to discover new storybooks.

1) Use a large piece of posterboard to make a colorful reading chart for your child.

2) At the top of the posterboard, write a title such as, "Andrew's Garden of Books" or "Katie's Sea of Stories." Use felt tip markers to add decorative details, such as green stems and leaves or blue waves.

3) From construction paper, cut flower or fish shapes of different colors.

4) Each time you and your child read a new book together, write the title on a flower or fish shape and let your child glue the shape on the posterboard chart.

5) Continue until the chart is filled with flowers or fish.

TALKING BOOK

This listening activity provides your child with his or her own recording of a favorite storybook.

1) Place a blank audio tape in a small tape recorder.

2) Select a simple storybook.

3) Tape-record your reading of the storybook. At the end of each page say, "It's time to turn the page now," or, "Please turn the page."

4) Show your child how to follow the words in the book while listening to the tape.

5) Let your child listen to the recorded story as often as he or she wishes.

LIBRARY AT-HOME FUN

AGES
3 to 5

YOU WILL TEACH
Language

YOU WILL NEED
audio tape
tape recorder
storybook

MY PICTURE BOOK

This prereading activity is always a favorite with young children.

LIBRARY AT-HOME FUN

—

AGES
2 to 5

—

YOU WILL TEACH
Language

—

YOU WILL NEED
stapler
white paper
construction paper
pen
old magazines
scissors (optional)
glue

1) Make a blank book by stapling together several pieces of white paper with a colored construction paper cover.

2) With your child, choose a book topic such as animals.

3) Write the title "My Animal Book" and your child's name on the cover.

4) Have your child look through old magazines and catalogs to find pictures of animals.

5) Let your child cut or tear out the pictures and glue them in his or her book.

6) As your child "reads" the book to you, write his or her words on the pages, if you wish.

AGE VARIATION: *Let younger children choose from precut pictures that you have placed in a box.*

SHELVING BOOKS

Encourage your child to organize his or her books with this classification activity.

1) Select a variety of your child's books.

2) Clear out a low shelf of a bookcase.

3) First, have your child arrange the books on the shelf by size.

4) Next, have your child arrange the books by color or by thickness.

5) Then, help your child arrange the books on the shelf by topic, such as animal books or books about transportation.

6) Which way of arranging the books does your child like best?

LETTER SEARCH

This activity helps develop letter recognition.

1) Take your child to the area of the store where press-on alphabet letters are displayed.

2) Ask your child to look for different letters, such as a *B*, an *N*, or a *U*.

3) Help your child find the letters in his or her name.

ANOTHER IDEA: *For a math activity, point out the press-on numbers, asking your child to find a 2, a 5, and so forth.*

TOOL RIDDLES

You and your child will enjoy this problem-solving activity.

1) Show your child where tools are displayed in the store.

2) Name several of the tools and talk about how they are used.

3) Make up a riddle about one of the tools. For example, say, "I pound in nails. I have a wooden handle. What am I?"

4) When your child answers the riddle, make up another one, or have your child make up a riddle for you to answer.

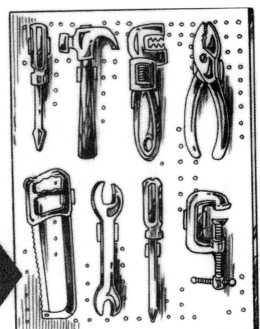

tools

BIGGEST AND SMALLEST

This comparison activity can also be done with nails, screws, and similar items.

1) At the store, show your child a display of tools, such as screwdrivers, that come in various sizes.

2) Ask your child to tell you which screwdriver is the biggest and which is smallest.

3) Follow the same procedure with other tools, such as wrenches and hammers.

ANOTHER IDEA: *Ask your child to point to the small, medium, and large size of a particular tool.*

SORTING SCREWS

Your child will use matching and sorting skills when doing this activity.

1) In the store, find a low row of four or five bins that contain screws of different sizes.

2) Remove one screw from each bin, mix them up, and give them to your child.

3) Help your child put each screw back into the bin that contains screws of the same size.

HARDWARE STORE COUNTING

A hardware store is a great place for doing math activities like this one.

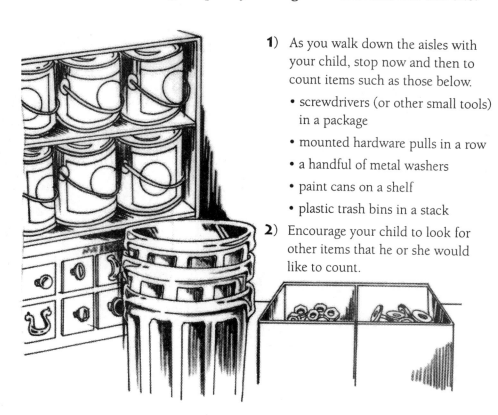

1) As you walk down the aisles with your child, stop now and then to count items such as those below.

- screwdrivers (or other small tools) in a package
- mounted hardware pulls in a row
- a handful of metal washers
- paint cans on a shelf
- plastic trash bins in a stack

2) Encourage your child to look for other items that he or she would like to count.

CHECKOUT-STAND GAME

This problem-solving activity helps stretch the imagination.

1) When you are waiting in line, show your child one of the hardware items in a small package hanging beside the checkout stand, such as an eyeglass repair kit.

2) Ask your child to guess what the item is and how it might be used.

3) Praise your child for his or her inventive answer—no matter what it is—before explaining what the item is actually used for.

HARDWARE STORE

—

AGES
4 to 5

—

YOU WILL TEACH
Thinking Skills

—

YOU WILL NEED
packaged hardware items

HOW DO THEY FIT?

This activity helps promote small-muscle development.

HARDWARE STORE

—

AGES
3 to 5

—

YOU WILL TEACH
Coordination

—

YOU WILL NEED
plastic fittings

1) In the plumbing section of the store, look for bins of plastic fittings.

2) Remove several of the fittings that go together.

3) Let your child practice screwing the fittings together and unscrewing them.

4) Have your child help you put the fittings back into the proper bins.

ANOTHER IDEA: *Follow the same procedure using extra-large nuts and bolts.*

COLORS AND FEELINGS

Try this self-esteem activity when you are in the paint section of the store.

1) Select paint sample strips of different colors.

2) Show the strips to your child.

3) Have your child tell you which colors make him or her feel happy, sad, excited, restful, and so forth.

4) Ask questions such as: "If you could paint the walls of your room any color you want, what color would you choose? What color would you paint the floor? The ceiling? The furniture?"

ANOTHER IDEA: *For a matching game, let your child help you put the paint sample strips back into the display case with the strips that contain matching colors.*

HARDWARE STORE

—

AGES
2 to 5

—

YOU WILL TEACH
Self-Awareness

—

YOU WILL NEED
paint sample strips

DOORMAT TEXTURES

This sensory-awareness activity involves recognition of different textures.

1) Take your child to the area of the store where doormats are displayed.

2) Arrange three doormats with different textures in a row on the floor.

3) Have your child touch the mats and tell you which feels smooth, soft, prickly, and so forth.

4) While your child closes his or her eyes, move the mats around and ask your child to try to identify them by touch.

5) Replace the doormats where you found them.

FIX-IT PERSON

This dramatic-play activity promotes coordination and thinking skills.

1) Select a sturdy box to use as a fix-it box for your child.

2) In the box, place items such as screwdrivers, large screws, softwood or plastic foam pieces, a tape measure, old locks and keys, broken toys, and masking tape.

3) Let your child pretend to be Mr. or Ms. Fix-It, and do such things as drive screws into the softwood or plastic foam pieces, measure furniture or other objects, match the locks and keys, and "repair" the broken toys with masking tape.

4) Can your child think of other "fix-it projects" to do? What about using a dry paintbrush to "paint" furniture?

HARDWARE STORE AT-HOME FUN

—

AGES
3 to 5

—

YOU WILL TEACH
Language

—

YOU WILL NEED
sturdy box
screwdrivers
large screws
softwood or plastic foam
tape measure
old locks and keys
broken toys
masking tape
paintbrush

COLOR SHADES

This ordering activity uses color-recognition skills

1) Bring home from a hardware store several paint sample strips of different colors.

2) Cut each shaded strip into separate color pieces and place the pieces of each strip in a separate envelope.

3) Let your child remove the color pieces from one envelope and arrange them in order from lightest to darkest.

4) Have your child follow the same procedure with the color pieces in the other envelopes.

5) Let your child put the pieces back into the envelopes to play with again another time.

HOME REPAIR SEQUENCE CARDS

Understanding what comes first, next, and last is the focus of this sequencing activity.

1) Select three index cards.

2) Using felt tip markers, draw three simple pictures on the cards that show the steps in repairing a broken table; for instance, a table with two legs, the same table with three legs, the table with four legs.

3) Make similar sets of sequence cards to show the steps in other home repair jobs, such as changing a light bulb or painting the front of a house.

4) Store each set of cards in a separate envelope.

5) To play, let your child remove the cards from an envelope and arrange them in the proper order.

HARDWARE STORE AT-HOME FUN

—

AGES
3 to 5

—

YOU WILL TEACH
Thinking Skills

—

YOU WILL NEED
index cards
felt tip markers
envelopes

NAPKIN PUPPET

This oral-language activity can be done at the restaurant while you are waiting to be served.

RESTAURANT

—

AGES
3 to 5

—

YOU WILL TEACH
Language

—

YOU WILL NEED
paper napkin
pen

1) To make a puppet, first cover your hand with a paper napkin.

2) Bring your thumb and fingers together and gently push in the napkin between them to form a mouth.

3) Let your child use a pen to add eyes and other details.

4) Use the puppet to talk to your child about what is going on at the restaurant, what you are going to order, and so forth.

ANOTHER IDEA: *Make a second Napkin Puppet for your child and have your puppets talk to each other.*

STRAW SOUNDS

Try this listening activity when you are at a fast-food restaurant.

1) Hold a drinking straw in a glass of water placed on the table.

2) Have your child listen as you blow across the top of the straw to make a sound.

3) Continue blowing as you lower the straw into the water. Ask your child to tell you what happens to the sound. (It becomes higher.)

4) Continue blowing as you raise the straw in the water. What happens to the sound now? (It becomes lower.)

5) Let your child try creating high and low sounds with his or her own glass of water and drinking straw.

PLACEMAT BOARD GAME

This matching activity can also be done with numbers or alphabet letters.

RESTAURANT

AGES
3 to 5

YOU WILL TEACH
Thinking Skills

YOU WILL NEED
*paper placemat or scrap paper
pen*

1) Use the back of a paper placemat or a piece of scrap paper to make a gameboard.

2) Down the left-hand side of the gameboard, draw a column of shapes, such as a circle, a square, a triangle, a rectangle, and a star.

3) Down the right-hand side, draw the same shapes in a different order.

4) Let your child draw lines on the gameboard to connect the matching shapes.

COASTER GAME

Your child helps make the game piece in this predicting activity.

1) Collect three paper coasters.

2) Let your child use a pen to draw a design on the back of one coaster.

3) Place the coasters on the table in a row, printed sides up. Lift the coaster with the design on it to show your child where it is.

4) Slowly move the coasters around to change their positions.

5) Ask your child to point to the coaster that has his or her design on the back.

6) Turn the coasters over and let your child check his or her response.

7) Let your child move the coasters around and have you guess which one has the design on the back.

AGE VARIATION: *Make only one move for younger children. Challenge older children with two or more moves.*

RESTAURANT

—

AGES
3 to 5

—

YOU WILL TEACH
Thinking Skills

—

YOU WILL NEED
paper coasters
pen

PLACE SETTING MATCH

Your child reproduces a pattern with this learning game.

RESTAURANT

AGES
3 to 5

YOU WILL TEACH
Thinking Skills

YOU WILL NEED
silverware
napkins

1) Sit next to your child at the restaurant table.

2) Arrange your knife, fork, spoon, and napkin in the proper places in front of you.

3) Place your child's silverware and napkin in a pile.

4) Ask your child to copy the arrangement of your place setting to create one for him- or herself.

ANOTHER IDEA: *Arrange silverware pieces in a place setting on the back of a paper placemat and trace around them with a pen. Let your child place the silverware on the matching tracings.*

PAPER WIGGLY WORM

This science activity is always entertaining for young children.

1) Stand a straw in its wrapper upright on the table.

2) Tear off the top of the wrapper.

3) Push the wrapper down around the straw as far as it will go.

4) Pull out the straw and set it aside, leaving the accordion-folded "worm" on the table.

5) Help your child shake one small drop of water at a time on the paper worm and watch as it "squirms" and "wiggles."

6) Explain that the drops of water make the tiny folds in the paper unfold, causing the wrapper to move around.

RESTAURANT

—

AGES
3 to 5

—

YOU WILL TEACH
Science

—

YOU WILL NEED
*wrapped drinking straw
water*

LET'S PLAY RESTAURANT

Your child will enjoy waiting tables with this dramatic-play activity.

**RESTAURANT
AT-HOME FUN**

AGES
3 to 5

YOU WILL TEACH
Language

YOU WILL NEED
*table
placemats
silverware
plates
cups
menu
pencil
notepad*

94

1) On a table, let your child arrange such items as placemats, silverware, plates, and cups to make a pretend restaurant.

2) Provide a real menu or use one that you and your child design yourselves.

3) With your child, take turns being the waiter or waitress and the customer, doing such things as "reading" the menu, "writing" pretend orders on a notepad, and serving and enjoying imaginary foods.

FAST-FOOD ORDERS

Listening to and following directions is the focus of this activity.

1) From a fast-food restaurant, collect several hamburger containers, paper cups, and French fry holders, or cut out paper shapes to represent the three items.

2) Place the containers and a paper bag on a table.

3) Give your child an "order" to fill, such as one burger, two soft drinks, and one fries.

4) Have your child repeat your order as he or she places the appropriate containers or paper shapes into the bag.

5) Remove the items from the bag and continue the game, letting your child take a turn giving you an order to fill.

AGE VARIATION: *For younger children, start by giving an order that includes just two items. For older children, include more items per order or ask for a larger number of each item.*

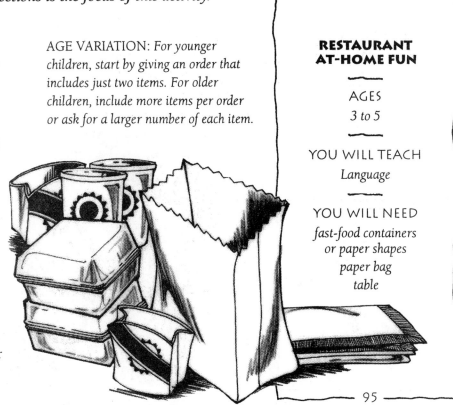

RESTAURANT AT-HOME FUN

———

AGES
3 to 5

———

YOU WILL TEACH
Language

———

YOU WILL NEED
*fast-food containers
or paper shapes
paper bag
table*

MEASURING SOFT DRINKS

This math activity provides an entertaining way to develop measuring skills.

RESTAURANT AT-HOME FUN

—

AGES
2 to 5

—

YOU WILL TEACH
Thinking Skills

—

YOU WILL NEED
paper cups
water
measuring cups

96

1) From a fast-food restaurant, collect a small, a medium, and a large paper cup (or use any small, medium, and large cups you have on hand).

2) Provide your child with water and a set of plastic measuring cups.

3) Let your child practice pouring and measuring to discover how much "soft drink" each cup holds.

COUNTING FRIES

This homemade math game can be used for various counting activities.

1) Collect two cardboard French fry holders of different sizes from a fast-food restaurant.

2) Using scissors, cut yellow sponges into French fry shapes.

3) Ask your child to count the number of fries that will fit into each holder.

4) Have your child remove the fries from each holder, counting as he or she does so.

5) Ask your child to fill each container with a specific number of fries.

6) Let your child make up other counting games to play using the fries and holders.

RESTAURANT AT-HOME FUN

—

AGES
3 to 5

—

YOU WILL TEACH
Thinking Skills

YOU WILL NEED
French fry holders
scissors
yellow sponges

FOODS ON PLATES

Learning to understand ordinal numbers is the focus of this math activity.

RESTAURANT AT-HOME FUN

AGES
3 to 5

YOU WILL TEACH
Thinking Skills

YOU WILL NEED
scissors
old magazines
paper plates

1) Cut pictures of foods from old magazines and give them to your child.

2) Place three to five paper plates in a row.

3) Talk with your child about the positions of the plates—which one is first, second, and so on.

4) Have your child place the food pictures on the plates as you give directions such as: "Put the apple on the second plate. Put the sandwich on the third plate. Put the cake on the first plate."

MAY I TAKE YOUR ORDER?

Use this activity to encourage self-esteem.

1) On a piece of paper, draw simple pictures of the beverages that will be offered at your next family meal.

2) After each picture, draw a box for each member of your family.

3) Give the "beverage menu" to your child.

4) At mealtime, have your child ask each person what drink he or she would like.

5) Have your child check off the drinks that each person requests.

6) Let your child bring the menu to the kitchen and help you prepare the beverages that were ordered.

RESTAURANT AT-HOME FUN

AGES
4 to 5

YOU WILL TEACH
Self-Awareness

YOU WILL NEED
paper
pen
beverages

GARDENING TOOLS GAME

This dramatic-play activity will help your child learn about how garden tools are used.

1) Take your child to the area in the store where gardening tools are displayed.

2) Point to a tool, such as a hoe or rake, and help your child say its name.

3) Talk about how the tool is used.

4) Have your child pretend to hold the tool and act out how he or she would use it in a garden.

BUYING A PLANT

Your child will enjoy doing this oral-language activity.

1) With your child, look at small plants that are on display in the store.

2) Let your child choose a plant to purchase and take home.

3) Teach your child the plant's name.

4) Have your child take the plant to the salesclerk and ask how to care for it at home.

5) Later, discuss with your child what the clerk said about taking care of the plant.

ANOTHER IDEA: *Make a weekly chart that shows when your plant should be watered. With your child, check off the task on the chart as you do it.*

GARDEN STORE

—

AGES
3 to 5

—

YOU WILL TEACH
Language

—

YOU WILL NEED
small plants
salesclerk

SEED PACKET FUN

Colorful seed packets are great to use for matching activities like this one.

1) At the store, take your child to the seed packet display.

2) Talk with your child about the pictures of different flowers and vegetables on the packets.

3) Have your child close his or her eyes while you remove one of the seed packets from the display case.

4) Ask your child to open his or her eyes.

5) Give your child the seed packet and have him or her put it back into the display case with the packets that contain matching pictures.

6) Follow the same procedure using other seed packets.

ANOTHER IDEA: *For a color-recognition game, have your child point to a seed packet that has a picture of red flowers, yellow squash, green lettuce, and so forth.*

HOW TALL?

Use this math activity to develop an understanding of measurements.

1) Take your child to the area of the store that contains tree saplings or bushes.

2) Have your child choose a sapling or bush and stand beside it.

3) Together, decide if the plant is taller, shorter, or the same height as your child.

4) Encourage your child to choose other saplings or bushes to stand beside and "measure."

5) When you are standing beside a sapling, ask your child to tell you if the plant is taller, shorter, or the same height as you are.

ANOTHER IDEA: *Let your child compare his or her height to various garden stakes.*

GARDEN STORE

AGES
2 to 5

YOU WILL TEACH
Thinking Skills

YOU WILL NEED
tree saplings or bushes

SEEDS AND PLANTS

Encourage your child's observation skills with this matching activity.

GARDEN STORE

AGES
3 to 5

YOU WILL TEACH
Thinking Skills

YOU WILL NEED
seed packets
plants

106

1) At the store, choose several seed packets that have pictures of plants that are on display.

2) With your child, take the packets to the plant area.

3) Select one of the seed packets and help your child find the growing plants that are pictured on it.

4) Follow the same procedure with the other packets.

5) When you have finished, replace the seed packets in the display case.

LITTLE SEED, BIG TREE

Try this whole-body movement activity in an outdoor area of the garden store.

1) With your child, find a tree sapling.

2) Talk with your child about how tall the tree will grow.

3) Have your child crouch down next to the sapling and pretend to be a tree seed deep in the ground.

4) As you "water" the seed and talk about how the warm sun is shining, have the seed "sprout" and begin to grow tall.

5) Continue talking about the growing tree as your child stands taller and taller, finally stretching out his or her arms for branches and wiggling his or her fingers for leaves or needles.

USING MY SENSES

This sensory-awareness activity is especially suited to a garden store.

GARDEN STORE

AGES
3 to 5

YOU WILL TEACH
Self-Awareness

YOU WILL NEED
garden store setting

1) Talk with your child about our five senses of sight, hearing, touch, smell, and taste.

2) Ask your child to look around and describe a special sight, such as a red geranium, for you.

3) Ask your child to listen and then name a sound, such as water flowing in a fountain.

4) Have your child touch and describe a textured item, such as a rough tree trunk or a smooth ceramic planter.

5) Can your child describe any scents, such as those given out by herbs or flowers?

6) Later, for a taste experience, let your child sample herbs that you have taken home and washed.

GARDENING BOX

This dramatic-play activity can be done either inside or outdoors.

1) Find a sturdy box.

2) In the box, place gardening items for your child to play with, such as a watering can, a trowel, gardening gloves, and empty seed packets.

3) Let your child use the gardening items to pretend he or she is planting a garden, watering the plants, and pulling weeds.

4) Ask your budding gardener to describe his or her garden for you.

GARDEN PLAN

Encourage your child's imagination with this art activity.

1) From old seed catalogs, let your child cut or tear pictures of flowers, vegetables, and other plants.

2) Give your child a piece of brown construction paper or wrapping paper to use as an empty garden bed.

3) Have your child try arranging the flower and vegetable pictures on the paper in different ways to come up with a "garden" he or she likes.

4) When your child is satisfied with an arrangement, let him or her glue the pictures in place on the paper.

5) Display the Garden Plan on a wall or door for everyone to admire.

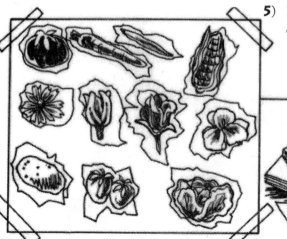

FLOWER POT FUN

This ordering activity is enjoyable and easy to do.

1) Find four to six plastic flower pots that fit together, one inside the other.

2) Let your child help wash and dry the pots.

3) Encourage your child to practice nesting the pots together and taking them apart again.

CITRUS SEED GARDENS

This natural science activity uses seeds of everyday fruits.

GARDEN STORE AT-HOME FUN

AGES
3 to 5

YOU WILL TEACH
Science

YOU WILL NEED
potting soil
flower pots
citrus fruit seeds
water

112

1) Have on hand potting soil and small flower pots.

2) Save several seeds from an orange, a lemon, or a grapefruit.

3) Help your child plant the seeds about 1 inch deep in a pot filled with potting soil. Gently add water.

4) Place the pot in a sunny spot, letting your child water the seeds a little every day.

5) Plant seeds from several different citrus fruits in separate pots and group them together to make a "garden."

HINT: *Do not let the seeds dry out before planting or they may not sprout.*

HOMEMADE TERRARIUM

Your child will enjoy growing plants in a different way with this natural science activity.

1) Put a layer of pebbles and 2 or 3 inches of potting soil in the bottom of a wide-mouthed glass or plastic jar.

2) Let your child help plant one or two small plants in the soil.

3) Have your child use a spoon to add a small amount of water to the plants.

4) Screw the lid on the jar.

5) Keep the terrarium in a spot where it will get plenty of light (but not in direct sunlight) and have your child observe as the plants grow.

6) Explain to your child that the water inside the terrarium is recycled over and over again so that no more water needs to be added.

HINT: *At first you may need to leave the lid off the jar for a while or add a little more water to get the right balance of moisture in the terrarium.*

ANOTHER IDEA: *Let your child place a small plastic or ceramic animal in the terrarium, if he or she wishes.*

FUN-TO-GROW PLANTS

This natural science activity offers ideas for growing edible plants.

**GARDEN STORE
AT-HOME FUN**

AGES
3 to 5

YOU WILL TEACH
Science

YOU WILL NEED
*garden or outside planter
lettuce seeds
spinach seeds
herb seeds
sunflower seeds*

1) Give your child space outdoors in a garden or planter to plant seeds that are easy to grow. Here are some suggestions.

   • Plant lettuce seeds along with spinach seeds to make a salad garden.

   • Grow several different herbs, such as oregano, chives, and thyme. Use the herbs in salads, on steamed vegetables, or on top of pizza.

   • Plant carrot and radish seeds to grow vegetables that taste terrific right out of the garden.

   • Plant sunflower seeds and watch the flowers grow to maturity. Harvest the seeds later.

2) Help your child care for his or her garden, watering and weeding as needed.

WHAT DO PLANTS NEED?

Try this science experiment to show that plants need sunlight in order to grow.

1) Let your child plant bean seeds in two pots of soil.

2) When the seeds have sprouted, let your child help place one pot in a sunny place, such as a window, and the other in a dark place, such as a closet.

3) Water both plants regularly.

4) After about two weeks, have your child compare the two plants. What has happened to the plant in the dark closet? (It has become pale and thin because it lacked sunlight.)

5) Let your child place the pale plant in a sunny spot, continue watering it, and observe over the coming days as it turns green.

ANOTHER IDEA: *Have your child grow two plants in a sunny spot and experiment with watering one but not the other. What happens to the unwatered plant? (It becomes droopy.) Start watering the second plant and watch it perk up.*

A PERFECT GIFT
This oral-language activity is easy and fun to do.

DEPARTMENT STORE

—

AGES
3 to 5

YOU WILL TEACH
Language

—

YOU WILL NEED
store displays

1) As you walk through the department store with your child, stop occasionally in an area that has an interesting display.

2) Ask your child a question such as, "What would be a perfect present for Grandma?" or, "What do you wish you could get Daddy for his birthday?"

3) Have your child look around to find something he or she thinks would be a good present for that person.

4) Encourage your child to explain his or her choice.

5) Start the game again by asking about another family member or friend.

PICTURE MATCH

Your child is sure to enjoy helping you shop with this matching activity.

1) Before going to the department store, cut pictures of several items you want to buy out of the store's advertising circular.

2) Glue each picture on a separate index card.

3) At the store, give the cards to your child.

4) When you arrive at the department where one of the items is sold, help your child use the card as a guide to find that item.

5) Continue in the same manner with the items pictured on the remaining cards.

DEPARTMENT STORE

AGES
3 to 5

YOU WILL TEACH
Thinking Skills

YOU WILL NEED
scissors
store advertising circular
glue
index cards
store displays

HOW IS IT USED?

You can do this classification activity in any department.

DEPARTMENT STORE

—

AGES
3 to 5

—

YOU WILL TEACH
Thinking Skills

—

YOU WILL NEED
store displays

—120—

1) Point out various items for sale in the store and ask your child questions such as the following.

   • "Would you bathe with this or use it to decorate a table?"

   • "Would you use this for holding flowers or for cooking a hamburger?"

   • "Would you wear this around your neck or around your waist?"

   • "Would you give this to a baby to play with or to a pet?"

2) Encourage your child to explain any "unusual" answers he or she gives.

WHAT GOES TOGETHER?

Try this color-recognition activity when you are shopping for clothes.

1) Pick out a shirt with blue (or any desired color) in it.

2) Show the shirt to your child and ask him or her to help you find a pair of blue pants to go with it.

3) As you hold the shirt next to different pairs of pants, talk about whether or not the blues in the two items really match.

4) If the shirt has another color in it, such as red, look for a pair of red pants that might also go with it.

5) If you purchase one or more of the outfits, let your child help you look for such items as socks or shoes to wear with it.

AGE VARIATION: *Ask younger children to look for such things as a red shirt, blue pants, green mittens, and so forth.*

ALIKE AND DIFFERENT

Watching TV becomes a learning game with this comparison activity.

DEPARTMENT STORE

AGES
3 to 5

YOU WILL TEACH
Thinking Skills

YOU WILL NEED
television displays

1) Take your child to the television department of the store.

2) Together, look at all the TVs on display.

3) Talk about how most of the sets are tuned into the same program, showing identical pictures on their screens.

4) Ask your child to point out the sets that are not tuned into that program but are showing different pictures.

ANOTHER IDEA: *As you look at various store items on display, such as watches, ask your child to tell you how they are alike and how they are different.*

WHICH SECTION?

Discovering how like items are grouped together is the focus of this classification activity.

1) Find a copy of the store's advertising circular and look through it with your child.

2) Point out how the circular is divided into different sections.

4) Ask your child to find the clothing section, the furniture section, and the jewelry section, for example.

5) Have your child name some of the items found in each section.

ANOTHER IDEA: *Ask your child to look through the circular for items of various colors or for different shapes.*

DEPARTMENT STORE

—

AGES
3 to 5

—

YOU WILL TEACH
Thinking Skills

—

YOU WILL NEED
store advertising circular

LET'S SEE

Developing observation skills is the focus of this activity.

1) As you walk with your child through the store, try playing a game of Let's See.

2) Stop in a department, such as the shoe department, and say, "Let's see if we can find some shoes with buckles."

3) When your child locates the shoes, suggest other kinds of shoes to search for, such as blue shoes, running shoes, or men's shoes.

4) Continue the game in other departments, searching for such items as yellow bath towels, winter jackets, gold jewelry, striped neckties, and wooden toys.

I AM SPECIAL

Try this activity to help develop your child's self-esteem.

1) At the store, have your child stand in front of a full-length mirror.

2) Stand behind your child.

3) Talk about what is unique and special about the child in the mirror.

4) Ask your child to blink his or her beautiful eyes, show his or her happy smile, flex his or her strong arm muscles, tap his or her dancing feet, and so forth.

DEPARTMENT STORE

—

AGES
2 to 5

—

YOU WILL TEACH
Self-Awareness

—

YOU WILL NEED
mirror

JUST FOR ME

Boosting self-esteem is the aim of this activity.

DEPARTMENT STORE

—

AGES
3 to 5

YOU WILL TEACH
Self-Awareness

—

YOU WILL NEED
children's clothing displays

1) Take your child to the department where you would buy his or her clothes.

2) Hold a sweater or other piece of clothing up to your child and say, "Is this too big? Too small? Just right?" Repeat with other items.

3) Show your child two different shirts or other items of clothing. Ask, "Which one do you like best? Why?"

4) As you walk around the clothing department, ask your child questions such as: "How do you feel when you wear this color? Shorts like these? A wool shirt like this one?"

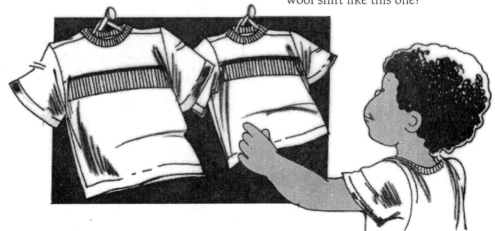

LET'S PLAY DEPARTMENT STORE

Dramatic-play activities like this one are always entertaining for young children.

1) Set out tables or boxes for your child to use to set up a pretend department store.

2) Give your child items to arrange for sale in the store, such as dress-up clothes, old jewelry, toys, doll dishes, and washcloths.

3) With your child, take turns being the store clerk and the customer, talking about the displayed items, buying and selling them with play money, and putting them into store bags to take "home."

ANOTHER IDEA: *For a coordination activity, provide tissue paper and tape and ask your child to gift-wrap items you "buy" at the store.*

DEPARTMENT STORE AT-HOME FUN

—

AGES
3 to 5

—

YOU WILL TEACH
Language

—

YOU WILL NEED
tables or boxes
dress-up clothes
old jewelry
toys
doll dishes
washcloths
play money
department store bags

SHOE DEPARTMENT FUN

You and your child are sure to enjoy this dramatic-play activity.

DEPARTMENT STORE AT-HOME FUN

—

AGES
3 to 5

—

YOU WILL TEACH
Language

—

YOU WILL NEED
shoes
shoeboxes

128

1) Let your child set up a pretend shoe department using pairs of his or her shoes and your shoes.

2) Have your child pair the shoes and put them into separate shoeboxes.

3) Pretend to be the customer and ask the "shoe clerk" for a pair of black shoes, running shoes, and so forth.

4) Let your child help you try on the shoes.

5) Pretend to buy the shoes when you find a pair you like.

6) Take the role of the shoe clerk and let your child be the customer.

FILLING TOY ORDERS

This activity involves listening to and following directions.

1) Let your child pretend to be a sales-clerk and arrange small toys on a table as if they were displayed in a store.

2) Give your child several store bags and a play telephone, or use a small flat box or other object as a phone prop.

3) Pretend to call in and place a phone order, such as two toy cars and one teddy bear.

4) Have your child fill the order by placing the toys in a bag.

5) Continue in the same manner giving other telephone orders.

6) Trade places and let your child place a telephone toy order for you to fill.

DEPARTMENT STORE AT-HOME FUN

AGES
4 to 5

YOU WILL TEACH
Language

YOU WILL NEED
small toys
table
department store bags
play telephone or prop

WHICH DEPARTMENT?

Your child will practice sorting skills with this activity.

1) Find a department store advertising circular.

2) From the circular, cut several pictures from each of four categories of goods, such as clothing, bath items, television sets, and toys.

3) Using a felt tip marker, divide a large piece of paper (like plain wrapping paper) into four sections.

4) Label the sections "Clothing Department," "Bath Department," "TV Department," and "Toy Department."

5) Give your child the cutout pictures and let him or her sort them into the appropriate sections.

ANOTHER IDEA: *When all the pictures have been sorted, let your child glue them in place to make a department store collage.*

SHOPPING GAME

This memory game can be played with more than two people.

1) Set out several items that can be found in a department store, such as a pair of socks, a small toy, a plastic bowl, a washcloth, and a piece of jewelry.

2) Name each of the items with your child.

3) Ask your child to close his or her eyes while you put one of the items into a paper sack.

4) When your child opens his or her eyes say, "I've been shopping, now I'm back. Can you guess what's in my sack?"

5) Have your child guess which item is missing and then look inside the sack to check his or her response.

6) Continue in the same manner until all the items have been used.

7) Start the game again and let your child be the "shopper."

DEPARTMENT STORE AT-HOME FUN

AGES
3 to 5

YOU WILL TEACH
Thinking Skills

YOU WILL NEED
*department store items
paper sack*

DOCTOR VISIT

Do this oral-language activity before your child's first visit to a doctor.

1) Make arrangements to take your child to the doctor's office for a "learning visit."

2) Ask to have someone show you and your child around the office and introduce the doctor and nurse.

3) Help your child prepare in advance any questions he or she may have for the doctor. Make sure any fears are addressed.

4) If possible, arrange for your child to receive a disposable face mask or similar item to take home.

5) Later, talk about the visit, asking your child to tell you some of the new things he or she learned at the doctor's office.

COUNTING FUN

This math activity provides an entertaining way to pass the time while you are waiting.

1) With your child, count objects and people in the doctor's waiting room. Here are some examples.

- number of chairs
- number of people waiting
- number of pictures on the wall
- number of magazines
- number of children's books

2) Can your child find other things to count?

PICTURE COLORS

This color-recognition activity involves observation skills.

DOCTOR'S OFFICE

AGES
3 to 5

YOU WILL TEACH
Thinking Skills

YOU WILL NEED
wall pictures

1) Call attention to a picture on the wall of the waiting room or examining room.

2) Talk with your child about what he or she sees in the picture.

3) Ask your child questions such as: "What color is the dog? Is the boat blue or green? What red things can you see in the picture? How many yellow things can you see?"

4) Encourage your child to ask you a color question about a picture on the wall.

WHICH IS BIGGER?

Play this comparing game while you are waiting with your child in the examining room.

1) Help your child name various items in the room, such as the examining table, scale, stethoscope, and tongue depressors.

2) Ask questions such as: "Which is bigger, the stethoscope or a tongue depressor? The examining table or the scale?"

3) Continue with questions about other items. For instance, ask: "Which is bigger, a baby or a nurse? A bed or a hospital? An ambulance or a bandage?"

4) Let your child make up similar questions for you to answer.

PARTS OF THE BODY

This body-awareness activity is very appropriate for the doctor's office.

DOCTOR'S OFFICE

—

AGES
2 to 5

—

YOU WILL TEACH
Self-Awareness

—

YOU WILL NEED
compact or hand mirror

1) Give your child a compact or hand mirror.

2) Have your child look in the mirror and point to parts of his or her face, such as eyes, nose, lips, and teeth, as you name them.

3) Name other body parts, one at a time, and have your child point to those parts.

ANOTHER IDEA: *With your child, find a picture of a person in a magazine. As you name different body parts, have your child point to them in the picture.*

DOCTOR/NURSE BAG

Your child takes the role of doctor or nurse with this dramatic-play activity.

1) Find an old shaving kit or purse for your child to use as a doctor or nurse bag.

2) Inside the bag, place a few medical items, such as adhesive bandages, gauze strips, tongue depressors, cotton swabs, and cotton balls.

3) Give your child the bag and let him or her act out being a doctor or nurse, treating you or toy animal "patients" for various pretend ailments.

AGE VARIATION: *Give older children notepads and pencils and encourage them to "write" prescriptions for their patients.*

DOCTOR'S OFFICE AT-HOME FUN

AGES
3 to 5

YOU WILL TEACH
Language

YOU WILL NEED
*old shaving kit or purse
adhesive bandages
gauze strips
tongue depressors
cotton swabs
cotton balls
toy animals*

PUPPET HEALTH TALK

Encourage good health habits while entertaining your child with this oral-language activity.

1) Select an old toothbrush, a bar of soap, an apple or orange, and a facial tissue.

2) Show your child the toothbrush and manipulate it like a puppet saying, "How do you use me to keep your teeth healthy?"

3) Let your child respond to the puppet's question.

4) Continue by having the soap bar "puppet" ask, "How do you use me to chase germs away?"

5) Next, have the apple or orange puppet ask, "How do you use me to keep your body healthy?"

6) Finally, have the facial tissue puppet ask, "How do you use me to keep cold germs from spreading?"

7) Give the puppets to your child and let him or her make up good-health stories for them to tell.

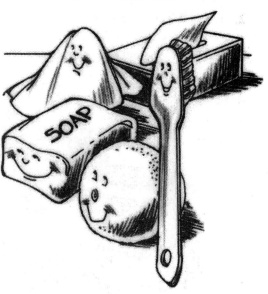

HELP FOR OUCHES
Your child will love this art activity.

1) Give your child a piece of construction paper along with crayons or felt tip markers.

2) Help your child draw a self-portrait with several "ouches" on its body.

3) Show your child how to unwrap some small adhesive bandages.

4) Let your child attach the bandages over the "ouches" in his or her picture.

GOOD-HEALTH POSTERS

This art activity helps reinforce good health habits.

1) Let your child make Good-Health Posters to put up in his or her room.

2) On separate pieces of construction paper, use a dark crayon to write the titles "I Wash My Hands," "I Brush My Teeth," and "I Use a Tissue."

3) Let your child use crayons to add decorations.

4) Have your child complete the posters by taping or gluing a soap bar wrapper to the first paper, a flattened toothpaste box to the second paper, and a facial tissue to the third paper.

5) Display the finished posters on a wall or door.

ANOTHER IDEA: *Title another poster "Do Not Touch!" and let your child decorate it with Mr. Yuk stickers. (Call your local poison control center or pharmacy to find out where to get the stickers in your area.)*

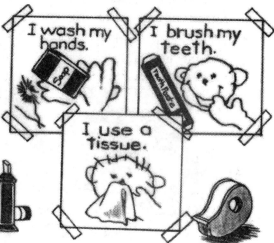

SHARING BOXES

Your child will learn good health habits with this sorting activity.

1) Using a felt tip marker, label one box with a happy face and the words "All right to share" and another box with a sad face and the words "Not healthy to share."

2) Collect several familiar items that are all right to share with friends, such as a ball, a crayon, a toy, and a book, and several items that are not healthy to share, such as a toothbrush, a cup, a comb, and a drinking straw.

3) Show your child two of the items, such as the ball and the toothbrush.

4) Talk about which item would not be healthy to share and why. (The toothbrush would not be healthy to share because it is something people put in their mouth.)

5) Mix up all the items and place them by the boxes.

6) Let your child choose one item at a time, tell you if it is all right to share or not, and then put the item into the appropriate box.

DOCTOR'S OFFICE AT-HOME FUN

AGES
3 to 5

YOU WILL TEACH
Thinking Skills

YOU WILL NEED
felt tip marker
boxes
items that are all right to share
items that are not healthy to share

BANDAGE PLAY

This activity helps promote small-muscle development.

**DOCTOR'S OFFICE
AT-HOME FUN**

—

AGES
4 to 5

—

YOU WILL TEACH
Coordination

—

YOU WILL NEED
*scissors
masking tape
table or chair
stuffed animal*

1) Make some adhesive "bandages" by cutting masking tape into short strips.

2) Lightly attach the ends of the pretend bandages to the edge of a table or chair seat.

3) Let your child remove the bandages and attach them to him- or herself, to you, or to a stuffed animal.

ANOTHER IDEA: *Show your child how to unwrap and apply real adhesive bandages to a knee, a hand, a teddy bear, and so forth.*

GOOD-HEALTH CALENDAR

Learning to take care of oneself helps develop self-esteem.

1) Using pen and paper, make a calendar page for one week that includes a space for a picture.

2) With your child, choose a good health habit that you want to practice.

3) Make up a sentence that describes the habit, such as "We eat healthy snacks," and write it on your calendar page.

4) Let your child decorate the calendar with crayons or felt tip markers.

5) At the end of each day, attach two star stickers to your calendar to show that you and your child practiced your good health habit.

6) Each week, make a new calendar page for good habits, such as going to bed on time, washing hands before meals, and getting plenty of exercise.

DOCTOR'S OFFICE AT-HOME FUN

AGES
3 to 5

YOU WILL TEACH
Self-Awareness

YOU WILL NEED
pen
paper
crayons or felt tip markers
star stickers

OPPOSITE TALK

Try this vocabulary-building activity when you are in the car at the gas station.

GAS STATION

—

AGES
3 to 5

—

YOU WILL TEACH
Language

—

YOU WILL NEED
car environment

1) Talk with your child about opposites as suggested in the sentences below.

   • The driver sits on the *left* side of the car and the passenger on the *right*.

   • Roll the windows *down*, then *up*.

   • The engine is in the *front* of the car, and the trunk is in the *back*.

   • When we clean the windows, they must be *closed*, not *open*.

2) Encourage your child to think of other opposites.

I SPY

This color-recognition game is always fun to play.

1) Choose a color such as black.

2) Say, "I spy, with my little eye, a black tire."

3) Ask your child to look out the window (or around the inside of the car) to find another black object, such as a truck.

4) Have your child say, "I spy, with my little eye, a black truck."

5) Continue the game, taking turns naming other black objects.

6) To start a new game, substitute a different color name for *black*.

GAS STATION

—

AGES
2 to 5

—

YOU WILL TEACH
Thinking Skills

—

YOU WILL NEED
gas station environment

FIRST TO LAST

A clean car is what you will have at the end of this sequencing activity.

1) Take your car through the car wash at the gas station.

2) Talk with your child about the order in which things happen, using such examples as the following.

   • First, the car goes into the car wash.

   • Second, the car is sprayed with plain water.

   • Third, the car is scrubbed with soapy water.

   • Fourth, the car is rinsed off.

   • Fifth, the car comes out of the car wash.

3) Later, ask your child to describe what happened at the car wash first, next, and so on.

GAS STATION COUNT

Do this math activity while sitting in the car.

1) With your child, look out through the car windows and count such items as those below.

- number of waiting cars
- number of doors on cars
- number of people inside cars
- number of gas pumps

2) Encourage your child to look for other items to count.

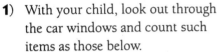

WINDOW CLEANER

This helping activity encourages large-muscle development.

GAS STATION

—

AGES
3 to 5

—

YOU WILL TEACH
Coordination

—

YOU WILL NEED
paper towel

1) Select one of the paper towels at the gas station used for washing windows.

2) Give the dry towel to your child.

3) Let your child use the towel inside the car to "wash" a nearby window, first pretending to squirt on soapy water, then wiping up and down and back and forth with the towel.

HOW MUCH?

Your child's self-esteem will blossom when doing this "grown-up" activity.

1) While gas is being pumped into your car, have your child watch the moving numbers on the pump.

2) When the tank is full, point out the numbers that tell how many gallons of gas were pumped and how many dollars they cost.

3) Point to the identification number on the gas pump and name it for your child.

4) Let your child go with you to the cashier, tell the cashier the pump number, and hand him or her the money for the gas.

GAS PUMP

Your child is sure to enjoy using this dramatic-play prop.

GAS STATION AT-HOME FUN

AGES
3 to 5

YOU WILL TEACH
Language

YOU WILL NEED
cardboard carton
sharp knife
old garden hose
tape
pistol-grip nozzle
felt tip markers
riding toys

1) Find a medium-sized cardboard carton to use to make a gas pump.

2) Turn the carton upside down and use a sharp knife to cut a small hole in one side.

3) Cut three to four feet off the end of an old garden hose.

4) Insert the cut end of the hose into the hole in the carton and tape it securely in place.

5) Attach a pistol-grip nozzle to the other end of the hose.

6) Let your child use the gas pump to "fill up" riding toys, encouraging him or her to talk about what is happening.

CAR MECHANIC

This dramatic-play activity uses prereading skills.

1) Cut several pictures of cars out of old magazines.

2) Glue the pictures on separate pieces of paper to make pretend work-order forms.

3) Attach the forms to a clipboard and give them to your child.

4) Have your child take the role of garage mechanic while you bring in a toy car to be "repaired."

5) As you name parts of the car for the mechanic to work on, such as a tire and a window, have your child use a pen to mark those parts on a work-order form picture.

6) When the "mechanic" is finished working, have him or her give back the car and "read" the work-order form to you, telling you what repairs were made.

7) Continue the game using other toy cars.

AGES
3 to 5

YOU WILL TEACH
Language

YOU WILL NEED
scissors
old magazines
glue
paper
clipboard
toy cars
pen

HOMEMADE ROAD MAP

This prereading activity is always a favorite with young children.

GAS STATION AT-HOME FUN

AGES
3 to 5

YOU WILL TEACH
Language

YOU WILL NEED
road map
large paper
toy cars
felt tip markers

1) Show your child a road map from the gas station and talk briefly about how a driver "reads" it.

2) On the floor, place a large piece of paper, such as brown wrapping paper.

3) Assemble some of your child's toy cars.

4) On the paper, use felt tip markers to draw a map with roads wide enough for the toy cars to travel on.

5) Add other details, such as pictures of houses, stores, a park, and a gas station.

6) Let your child "drive" the toy cars on the roads as you give directions such as: "Drive straight ahead to the park. Now turn and drive by the blue house. Stop when you get to the yellow store on the corner."

7) Let your child continue driving cars on the map any way he or she wishes.

NEIGHBORHOOD CAR WASH

Encouraging large-muscle development is the focus of this activity.

1) Help your child set up a Neighborhood Car Wash on the sidewalk or in your driveway.

2) Hook up a garden hose and set out buckets, rags, and sponges.

3) Have your child invite friends to bring over their riding toys.

4) Let the children use the hose, buckets, rags, and sponges to wash their "cars."

ANOTHER IDEA: *Let your child help you wash your car, using just water or a mild soap that is appropriate for young children.*

AGES
3 to 5

YOU WILL TEACH
Coordination

YOU WILL NEED
garden hose
buckets
rags
sponges
friends with riding toys

INDEX

About Me 65
Alike and Different 122
Apple Products 19
Arranging Letters 31
Bagging Groceries 23
Bakery Fun 16
Bandage Play 144
Bank Slips 45
Biggest and Smallest 76
Book Bingo 64
Book Pile 63
Book Questions 60
Book Stories 59
Buying and Selling 22
Buying a Plant 103
Car Mechanic 155
Checkout-Stand Game 79
Citrus Seed Gardens 112
Coaster Game 91
Coin Purse Game 53
Colorful Shopping 14
Colors and Feelings 81
Color Search 61
Color Shades 84
Counting Fries 97
Counting Fun 135
Counting in Line 49
Coupon Match 10

Deposit and Withdraw 44
Doctor/Nurse Bag 139
Doctor Visit 134
Dollar Bill Fun 46
Doormat Textures 82
Fast-Food Orders 95
Filling Toy Orders 129
First to Last 150
Fix-It Person 83
Flower Pot Fun 111
Foods on Plates 98
Fun in Line 30
Fun-to-Grow Plants 114
Gardening Box 109
Gardening Tools Game .. 102
Garden Plan 110
Gas Pump 154
Gas Station Count 151
Good-Health Calendar .. 145
Good-Health Posters 142
Grocery Picture List 8
Hardware Store
    Counting 78
Help for Ouches 141
Homemade Road Map .. 156
Homemade Terrarium ... 113
Home Repair Sequence
    Cards 85

How Do They Fit? 80
How Is It Used? 120
How Many Inside? 15
How Much? 153
How Tall? 105
I Am Special 125
In-Cart Waiting Games 17
I See Something 18
I Spy 149
Just for Me 126
Large and Small 12
Let's Play Bank 52
Let's Play
    Department Store 127
Let's Play Grocery Store 20
Let's Play Library 66
Let's Play Post Office 34
Let's Play Restaurant 94
Let's See 124
Let's Weigh Them 13
Letter Balance 33
Letter Search 74
Letters Everywhere 9
Little Seed, Big Tree 107
Loud and Soft 58
Mail Bag 35
Mailbox Fun 36
Mailbox Sorting Game 39

Mail Matchups 38
May I Take Your Order? ... 99
Measuring Soft Drinks 96
My Own Account 51
My Own Bank 55
My Own Mailbox 41
My Picture Book 70
Naming Coins 47
Napkin Puppet 88
Neighborhood
    Car Wash 157
Number Search 48
Opposite Talk 148
Page Count 62
Paper Wiggly Worm 93
Parts of the Body 138
Perfect Gift, A 118
Picture Colors 136
Picture Match 119
Placemat Board Game 90
Place Setting Match 92
Playdough Bakery 21
Postcards to Mail 26
Postcard Stories 27
Puppet Health Talk 140
Reading Corner 67
Read Me a Story 68
Ready to Mail 32

Seed Packet Fun 104
Seeds and Plants 106
Sharing Boxes 143
Shelving Books 71
Shining Pennies 54
Shoe Department Fun ... 128
Shopping Game 131
Sorting Screws 77
Stamp Descriptions 28
Stamp Lotto 40
Stamp Pictures 37
Straw Sounds 89
Talking Book 69
Tool Riddles 75
Using My Senses 108
What Doesn't Belong? 50
What Do Plants Need? ... 115
What Goes Together? 121
Where Would It Be? 11
Which Department? 130
Which Is Bigger? 137
Which Is Heavier? 29
Which Section? 123
Window Cleaner 152

Totline Teaching Tales are stories for sharing!

The front part of these children's books contains a wonderful tale that is delightfully illustrated in full color. The back of each book expands upon the themes of the story with related activity ideas: songs, poems, recipes, art, and movement!

Children ages 2 to 5 will enjoy the books as "read-alouds."

Children ages 6 to 8 can use the books as "easy-readers" and will be able to follow the simple instructions for the activities mostly on their own.

Kids Celebrate the Alphabet

Themes: Letters, Occupations
Jean Warren's newest children's story is told in rhyming verse. The beautiful, antibias art captivates children as well as adults. Encourage children to find the occupations featured on each page. Related activity pages follow the story. 32 pp.
Paperback WPH 1931

NATURE SERIES

These wonderful stories by Jean Warren focus on unique environments in nature. Filled with captivating illustrations, each story lets nature tell a gentle lesson. Related activities and songs ensure hours of fun. Each 32 pp.

Ellie the Evergreen

Themes: Fall, Winter, Self-Esteem
When the trees in the park turn beautiful colors in the fall, Ellie the Evergreen feels left out—until something special happens to her too.
Paperback WPH 1901 • Hardback WPH 1902

The Wishing Fish

Themes: Trees, North & South, Hot & Cold
A palm tree and a fir tree each get their wish to move to a different climate—thanks to the magical powers of the rainbow Wishing Fish.
Paperback WPH 1903 • Hardback WPH 1904

The Bear and the Mountain

Themes: Bears, Flowers, Friendship
Feel the joy of friendship as a playful bear cub and a lonely mountain get to know each other through the seasons of the year.
Paperback WPH 1905 • Hardback WPH 1906

✦✦✦ **Totline® Books are available at parent and teacher stores**

Great Resources for Parents!

TEACHING HOUSE₍ SERIES

This new series from Totline₍ Publications helps parents become aware of the everyday opportunities for teaching their children. The tools for learning are all around the house and everywhere you go. Easy-to-follow directions for using ordinary materials combine family fun with learning. Teach your child about language, art, science, math, problem-solving, self-esteem—and more!

Teaching House
Let *Teaching House* show you how to have fun in your own home while your child learns about language, art, science, math, problem-solving, and self-esteem. 160 pp.
WPH 2801

Teaching Town
While you are running errands around town, you can help your child learn important concepts. The tools for teaching your child are waiting for you at every corner! 160 pp.
WPH 2802

Teaching Trips
This excellent parent resource provides ideas for turning short day trips into learning experiences for preschoolers. Easy-to-follow directions combine family fun with learning. 160 pp.
WPH 2803

✱✱✱ **Totline₍ Books are available at parent and teacher stores**